Seasons

SPRING

Belitha Press

Anna Claybourne • *Pictures by Stephen Lewis*

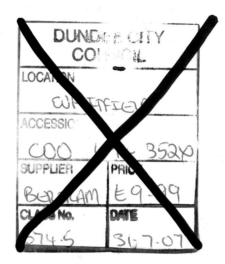

Belitha Press

First published in the UK in 2001 by
Belitha Press Limited, London House,
Great Eastern Wharf, Parkgate Road,
London SW11 4NQ

Copyright © Belitha Press Limited 2001
Text by Anna Claybourne

ISBN 1 84138 320 1

British Library Cataloguing in Publication Data
for this book is available from the British Library.

Printed in Hong Kong

10 9 8 7 6 5 4 3 2 1

Editor: Veronica Ross
Designer: Kathryn Caulfield
Illustrator: Stephen Lewis
Picture researcher: Diana Morris
Consultant: Elizabeth Atkinson

Photo credits

Damien Bree/Britstock-IFA: 22cr. Gay Bumgarner/Stone: 14b.
W. Perry Conway/Corbis: 15b. Peter Dean/Stone: 17tl.
Donna Disario/Stockmarket/Corbis: 13tl. Jack Dykinga/Stone: 9t.
Edinburgh Photographic Library: 23tr. Ron Giling/Still Pictures: 8b.
Ken Graham/Stone: 29tr. Haga/Britstock-IFA: 20bl, 22bl.
George Lepp/Stone: 5tl. Muzlish/Trip: 21tr.
Frank Oberle/Stone: 25tl. Hans Reinhard/Bruce Coleman Collection: 7t.
H Rodgers/Trip: 20t. T de Salis/Still Pictures: 12tl.
Pete Saloutos/Stockmarket/Corbis: 6b, 26tl.
Reinhard Siegel/Stone: 7b. Ariel Skelley/Stockmarket/Corbis: front cover,
16tr, 19tr.
Hans Strand/Stone: 11tr. Bob Thomas/Stone: 19tl.
Randy M Ury/Stockmarket/Corbis: 5cr.
A & J Verkaik/Stockmarket/Corbis: 24tl.
Kennan Ward/Stockmarket/Corbis: 10cl.

Every attempt has been made to clear copyrights but should there be
inadvertent omissions please apply to the publisher for rectification.

Contents

Words in **bold** are explained
on pages 30 and 31.

What is spring?

Spring is the time of year when the weather becomes warmer and the days grow longer. The sun shines more often and plants start to grow.

Most people like spring. The good weather makes everyone feel like going outside.

Spring is one of the four seasons: spring, summer, autumn and winter.

Together the four seasons make up a year.

Summer

Spring

4

In spring, new green leaves appear on the trees. Bees buzz from flower to flower collecting **pollen**.

Caterpillars munch their way through the new leaves, and animals that have spent the winter asleep wake up.

Autumn

Winter

A white-tailed deer with her fawn.

spring fact

Many animals have their young in spring. This is because there is plenty of sunshine and food to help them grow.

How spring happens

Why do we have seasons? Why isn't the weather the same all year round? The answer is because the Earth is tilted. The Earth's tilt doesn't change. But as the Earth travels around the Sun, the tilt makes the seasons change.

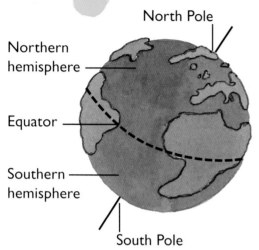

North Pole

Northern hemisphere

Equator

Southern hemisphere

South Pole

The Earth is tilted to one side. The **equator** divides the Earth into two halves, or hemispheres.

This picture shows the seasons in the **northern hemisphere**.

In summer, your part of the world is tilted towards the Sun, and the days are long and sunny.

Summer

Dogs love to play outside in the spring sunshine.

spring fact

In spring, the Sun appears higher in the sky every day.

Spring happens as the Earth moves around from winter to summer. There is more sunlight as your part of the world starts to lean towards the Sun.

Tulips, snowdrops, harebells and many other garden flowers start to bloom in spring.

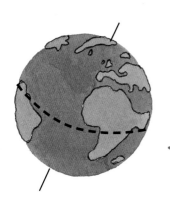

Spring

Sun

Winter

When your part of the world is tilted away from the Sun, there isn't much sunlight and the weather is cold. This is winter!

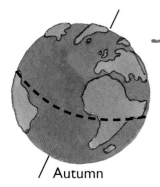

Autumn

Autumn happens when summer is turning into winter and there is less sunlight.

Yellow spring crocuses peep through the snow.

7

Around the world

Spring starts in September in **southern hemisphere** countries, such as Chile, Australia and New Zealand. In the northern hemisphere, spring begins in March. Wherever spring is happening, it is autumn on the opposite side of the world.

North Pole

Equator

South Pole

Spring comes later if you live near the **North** or **South Poles**, where the weather is always cold.

A farm worker at the equator in Uganda.

EQUATOR

N S

Spring comes earlier if you live near the equator, an imaginary line around the middle of the Earth.

spring fact

People who live right on the equator do not have seasons like the rest of the world. For them, it is hot and sunny nearly all the time.

Flowers bloom in an American desert after a spring rainfall.

When spring arrives in Japan, people hold picnic parties to welcome the blossoms on cherry and plum trees.

Spring weather

The Sun shines all year round, but spring feels warmer than winter. This is because the Earth tilts us a little bit nearer to the Sun in spring. Also, the days are longer and the Sun has more time to warm us up.

Icicles drip, drip, drip until they have disappeared.

Spring weather changes a lot. It can be windy...

Hard, frozen ground warms up, becoming soft, damp and perfect for plants.

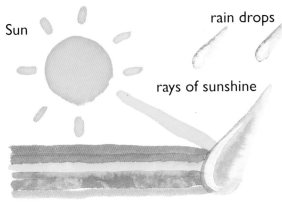

Sun

rain drops

rays of sunshine

coloured light

You often see **rainbows** in spring. They happen when bright sunshine hits falling rain. The Sun's **rays** bounce in and out of each raindrop. As the rays bend, they split up into different colours.

Spring sunshine makes winter snow and ice start to warm up. Snow on the mountains melts, filling streams and rivers with extra water.

...rainy...

...or bright and sunny!

If there is a rainbow, you will see it best if you stand with your back to the sun.

Plants in spring

Bluebells growing in a wood in springtime.

Plants **sense** the extra light and warmth in spring, and start to grow. That is why spring is so green and bright. Plants that seemed dead in winter come to life again.

Some plants, such as daffodils, spend the winter as **bulbs** under the ground. When spring comes shoots pop up out of the soil again.

Seeds that have been lying in the soil all winter **germinate** and push out roots and shoots.

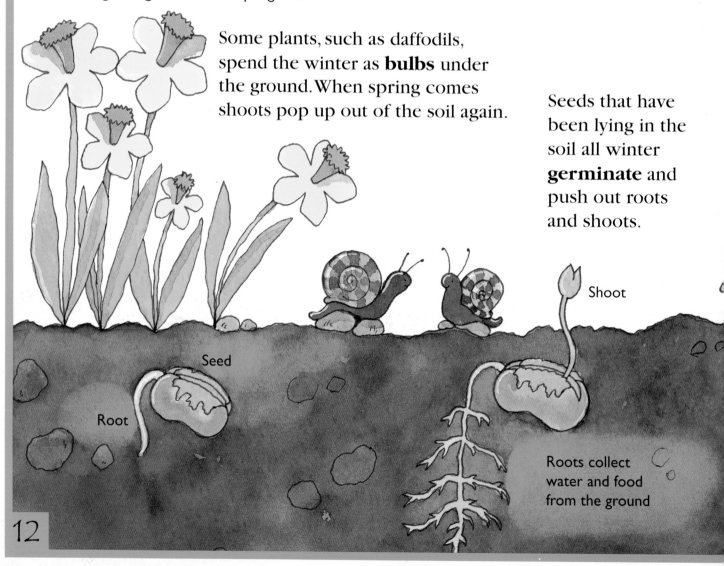

Shoot

Seed

Root

Roots collect water and food from the ground

12

Most trees have no leaves in winter, just tiny **buds**. When the buds feel the spring sunshine, they open out into new leaves.

Leaf

Animals in spring

In spring, many animals stop **hibernating**. They wake up from a long winter sleep and come outside.

A marmot eating flowers.

spring fact

When marmots wake up after hibernating, they weigh much less than in the autumn. This is because they do not eat all winter.

In North America, bears come out of their caves or underground dens in spring.

Birds lay eggs in spring. They collect twigs and build nests to lay their eggs in.

Some birds **migrate** to warmer countries for the winter. In spring, they fly back again.

The mother bird sits on the eggs to keep them warm.

After a few weeks, chicks **hatch** out of the eggs.

A female **lynx** has a litter of kittens every spring.

Animals such as rabbits, cats and dogs are **mammals**. They have babies instead of laying eggs.

On the farm

Spring is an important time for farmers. They have to plant new crops and help their animals have babies.

Cows spend the winter indoors, but in spring they go outside again and chew the fresh grass.

Sheep farmers are really busy in spring. This is when sheep have their lambs.

When the ground is soft and damp it is a good time to plant barley seeds and potatoes. The crops will grow bigger in summer and autumn.

When the weather becomes warmer, farmers shear the wool off their sheep. It doesn't hurt – it just helps the sheep stay cool.

People in spring

Most people love the spring. Your brain can sense the extra spring sunlight. It makes **hormones** (chemicals) that make you feel happy and give you energy.

As the weather becomes warmer, people put away their winter coats. New, brightly-coloured clothes appear in the shops, ready for summer.

Many people spring-clean their houses. They throw out rubbish and open the windows to let in the fresh air.

Gardeners clear up the last few dead leaves and plant new seeds.

18

People have important jobs to do in spring. They plant seeds, clear away rubbish and repaint buildings.

Seeds grow into tiny plants called seedlings.

Paint needs dry, warm weather to dry properly.

spring fact

Lots of sports seasons, such as baseball and horse racing, start in the spring.

Spring festivals

These children in Greece are dressed up for a parade on Good Friday, the Friday before Easter.

Spring **festivals** celebrate the new life of spring. Easter is a spring festival for **Christians**. It celebrates the time when Christ, leader of the Christians, rose from the dead.

Eggs are a symbol of spring and new life. That's why we eat chocolate eggs at Easter.

The Indian festival of Holi is a holiday for everyone. People run around the streets squirting each other with coloured water.

Passover is a festival for members of the Jewish religion. It takes place in March or April, and celebrates the time when God helped the Jews escape from slavery in Egypt.

On the night they escaped, the Jews didn't have time to make proper bread, so they made hard, flat bread instead. At Passover, Jews celebrate this by eating biscuits called matzohs.

At Passover, the youngest family member reads from a book called the Haggadah.

Egg-rolling contests are an Easter **tradition**. People roll the eggs down a slope or along the ground. The person whose egg goes furthest is the winner.

spring fact

In many countries, 1 April is April Fool's Day, when people play tricks on each other for fun.

Spring long ago

Long ago, during the cold winter months, people lived on dried food they had stored away. By the end of winter supplies were running low. Once spring came, they had enough food again.

Sometimes, after a bad harvest, people ran out of food during the winter.

Spring was a big festival for the ancient Egyptians. They watched the sun rise over a huge statue called the Sphinx, and made offerings of fresh spring **asparagus** to their gods.

The Sphinx still stands in Egypt today.

In the Middle ages, 1 May was celebrated by dancing round a **maypole**.

A modern maypole dance in England.

The **Celts** lived in Europe around 3000 years ago. They held a feast called **Beltane** on 1 May to welcome spring.

A recreation of Beltane in Scotland.

spring fact

The Easter bunny comes from an ancient spring festival. Long ago it was a **symbol** of new life, because rabbits have lots of babies.

At dawn on 1 May, girls washed their faces in **dew** to make themselves beautiful.

Spring dangers

Spring is often warm and sunny, but it can bring bad weather. In America, spring is the **tornado** season. Tornadoes are huge, spiralling windstorms that form when hot and cold winds mix together.

A tornado looks like a huge elephant's trunk reaching down from the sky.

spring fact

The wind in a tornado is the fastest in the world. It can blow as fast as 480 kilometres an hour.

In Russia, people go **ice fishing** on frozen lakes. In spring, the ice begins to thaw and break into chunks. Sometimes people are carried away on the pieces of ice, and have to be rescued!

In spring, warm sun melts winter snow and ice. Sometimes this causes flooding.

When **floods** are very deep, people can only escape from their houses by boat!

Spring activities

In spring, there are lots of things to see and do.

Be careful not to fall in the water!

Feed the ducks

Do you have a local duckpond, or a river where ducks live? Go with a grown-up to feed the **ducklings**. They like stale bread. Watch how fast they race to get the crumbs.

Decorating Easter eggs

Ask an adult to hard-boil some eggs for you. When they are cool, colour them with felt-tip pens.

Try drawing stripes, zigzags, spots or a face. Stick on some string or wool for hair.

Mother's Day

You can buy Mother's Day cards, but why not make one for your mum? You will need a piece of card and some paints or crayons.

Fold the piece of card in half. Draw or paint a beautiful spring picture and write a message inside.

Spring experiments

Try these experiments to find out about spring weather and plants.

Spring in a jar

If spring has not arrived yet, see if you can make it come early. Find a small twig from a tree – maybe from your garden. (If it is from someone else's garden, ask first!)

Put the twig in a jar of water and keep it in a warm place. If you can, put it on a sunny windowsill. Can you make the leaves come out before they come out on the trees outside?

Make a rainbow

On a bright sunny day, try making
a mini-rainbow outdoors. You need
a garden hose or a garden spray
bottle (ask an adult to help you).
Use the hose or the bottle to make
a fine spray of water in the air. Stand
with your back to the sun. See if
you can spot the colours of a
rainbow in the spray.

You probably won't make a rainbow this big!

29

Words to remember

bulb
A type of fat, round root that some plants have.

Celts
People who lived in parts of Europe in Ancient times, before the Romans.

Christian
A member of the Christian religion. Christians believe in Jesus Christ and have one god.

asparagus
A spring vegetable which has long green stalks.

Beltane
A festival held to celebrate spring.

bud
The part of a plant that grows into a flower or leaf.

dew
Drops of water which collect on the grass overnight.

duckling
A baby duck.

equator
The line around the middle of the Earth. There is no real line there – it is drawn on maps and globes.

festival
A party or feast to celebrate a special date.

flood
An overflow of water from a river or heavy rain.

germinate
When a seed germinates, it starts to grow.

hatch
To come out of an egg.

hibernate
To spend the winter asleep. Many animals hibernate.

hormone
A chemical that's made inside your body.

ice fishing
Dangling a fishing line through a hole carved in thick ice.

icicle
A long stick of ice, made by water freezing as it drips.

lynx
A kind of big cat.

mammal
A kind of animal. Mammals are usually furry and feed their young on milk.

maypole
A tall pole which people used to dance around on Mayday (1 May).

migrate
To travel to another place for part of the year.

northern hemisphere
The northern half of the world, where Europe, America and Russia are.

North Pole
The most northern point on Earth.

pollen
A yellow dust made by flowers.

rainbow
A curved ring of colours in the sky, made by sunlight shining on raindrops.

rays
Lines or beams of sunlight.

sense
To have a feeling about something.

southern hemisphere
The southern half of the world, where Australia is.

South Pole
The most southern point on Earth.

symbol
A sign that stands for something.

tornado
A kind of very strong windstorm.

tradition
Something people have done for a long time.

Index